AMERICA AT WAR

THE VIETNAM WAR

12 THINGS TO KNOW

I0794612

BLACK RABBIT BOOKS

LORI DITTMER

Table of Contents

Vietnam, Laos, and Cambodia were under French control until 1954.

Nations Fight for Control *of Vietnam*

1

World War II (1939–1945) left countries everywhere in pieces. The war's damage was huge. France scraped through on the side of the Allies. But it had lost control of its colonies in Asia. These colonies included Vietnam, Laos, and Cambodia. They were known as French Indochina. After the war, France tried to reclaim these areas.

In Vietnam, many people no longer wanted to live under French rule. Leader Ho Chi Minh led a **revolution**. He was a **communist**. He declared Vietnam's independence in 1945. France was against this. The First Indochina War started in 1946.

The United States was against communism. President Harry Truman wanted to stop its spread. He supported France. The United States sent the French guns and supplies. Ho Chi Minh's army was called the Viet Minh. China was another communist country. They helped the Viet Minh.

The war raged until 1954. France surrendered. France and Vietnam signed peace agreements. Vietnam became two independent countries. North Vietnam was communist. South Vietnam was not. The split was meant to be temporary. Elections were to be held in 1956. Leaders hoped to reunite the two nations.

North Vietnam President Ho Chi Menh

US President Harry Truman

GROWING INFLUENCE

Before World War I (1914–1918), the United States was neutral. It kept out of wars in other parts of the world. But after WWII, communist governments began to form. President Truman created a new policy. It was against communism. The US wanted to help spread democracy. To do so, it would help other countries.

17 Degrees north from equator that divides North and South Vietnam.

This line is called the 17th Parallel. • Leaders met in Geneva, Switzerland to settle the First Indochina War. • The plan became known as the Geneva Accords. • Peace agreements were signed on July 20 and 21, 1954.

Ho Chi Minh Forms a *Communist Vietnam*

2

Ho Chi Minh ruled North Vietnam. He did not allow non-communist groups there. He made many changes. These were meant to create fairness. Instead, they were used to treat people poorly.

One change was a land **reform** program. It started in 1953. The government took land from the people who owned it. Then, they gave it to the poor. Landlords were shamed in public. Their things were taken. Many were forced into labor camps. They were beaten. About 15,000 landowners were killed. Thousands more were sent away or put in prison.

Minh hoped to unite Vietnam. He wanted to control both the north and south. But the 1956 elections never took place. Ngo Dinh Diem led South Vietnam. He was the president. Diem refused to take part in the election. The United States supported him.

10,000 Estimated number of Viet Cong by 1960.

The Viet Cong began as a group opposed to Ngo Dinh Diem. • They received weapons and advice from North Vietnam. • During the 1960s, the number of Viet Cong soldiers grew quickly.

Paratroopers drop near a riverbank for a naval-land operation during the First Indochina War.

South Vietnam President Diem

That same year, Diem ended local elections in his own country. He got rid of political rivals. People did not like Diem. Many turned against him. Diem called them the Viet Cong. The name was short for "Viet Nam Cong San." In English, this means "Vietnamese Communists." The Viet Cong continued to grow. They threatened Diem's government.

The Liberation Army held a military parade after Ho Chi Minh took power in 1945.

A LEADER FOR VIETNAM Nguyen Tat Thanh was born on May 19, 1890. He left Vietnam in 1911 to find work. He lived on a ship and worked as a cook. He spent two years in London. Then he moved to France. He joined the French Communist Party in 1920. He traveled to Moscow to study communism. After WWII, he returned home. He helped to start the Viet Minh. He also took a new name, Ho Chi Minh. It means "Bringer of Light."

US Presidents Follow *Truman's Lead*

3

In 1947, President Truman began helping nations threatened by communism. This was called the Truman **Doctrine**. This sparked the beginning of the Cold War. The United States based its actions in Vietnam on this policy.

US presidents after Truman also supported South Vietnam. In 1955, Dwight D. Eisenhower sent advisers. They helped Ngo Dinh Diem control his country. Later, John F. Kennedy expanded US **aid**. He believed that if one country fell under communist rule, others would do the same thing.

President Kennedy

In 1962, Kennedy sent military advisers. They trained the South Vietnamese army. The US government claimed it had no military forces in Vietnam. But it kept sending in men. By the summer of 1963, there were more than 15,000 "advisers."

Kennedy was **assassinated** in November 1963. Lyndon B. Johnson became president afterward. The United States became much more involved in Vietnam. Johnson did not want to go to war. But he wanted to honor Kennedy's plans.

In August 1964, Johnson received a report. The North Vietnamese had attacked two US destroyer ships. Johnson sent **air strikes** on military bases along the North Vietnamese coastline. He sent more troops too. By 1965, more than 50,000 US soldiers were in Vietnam. Soviet Union was on North Vietnam's side. It sent weapons, supplies, and other equipment.

Vietnamese Aero L-39C Albatros

45 Number of years the Cold War lasted.

The Cold War was a political rivalry between the United States and Soviet Union. • The Soviet Union was a communist nation. • The Cold War ended in 1991.

THINK ABOUT IT

Why were US leaders worried about communism? How did this fear affect Americans' way of life?

Tonkin Incident Leads to *Military Action*

4

The US Navy had ships off the coast of North Vietnam. They were in **international waters**. In the summer of 1964, some were sent to the Gulf of Tonkin. One was the USS *Maddox*. Its job was to listen for communication between North Vietnamese vessels.

On August 2, boats from North Vietnam approached. The *Maddox* fired warning shots. The other boats sent torpedoes. The *Maddox* escaped. Another American ship, the *C. Turner Joy*, arrived. It was there as backup. Two days later, President Johnson received a message. It said both ships had been attacked.

Johnson sent air strikes against North Vietnam. Then he spoke to the US Congress. He called the attack an "open aggression on the high seas." He called for the power to use military action. Congress granted it. The Gulf of

2 Number of senators who voted against the Gulf of Tonkin **Resolution**.

President Johnson signed the resolution on August 10, 1964. • All 414 members of the House of Representatives voted for it. • It led to the United States directly entering the war in Vietnam.

A warship launches a torpedo.

Tonkin Resolution was approved. It gave Johnson more power. It allowed him to use armed force in Vietnam.

Later, a more detailed report showed that there had not been a second attack. The first message had been a mistake. But Johnson was under pressure to do more in the war. He felt like he was forced to act. The resolution was not an official declaration of war. But it was treated as such. The US military acted quickly. In February 1965, the United States began bombings in North Vietnam.

THINK ABOUT IT

President Johnson called for war after a serious attack. Do you think this was an acceptable reason? Is war always a just solution?

The USS Maddox *was only slightly damaged from the incident.*

5 US Relies on Helicopters *in Vietnam*

In past wars, helicopters had not been used much. They were heavy and slow. New technology made helicopters lighter. They were faster. They could fly in and out of tight spaces. In Vietnam, every branch of the US military used them.

Helicopters changed the way wars were fought. In the past, ground forces had limited speed. Soldiers could go only as far as they could walk. Rivers and mountains slowed them down.

Helicopters could drop soldiers directly into battle. They could also be dropped behind enemy lines. This meant they could attack from both sides. They could cut off enemy troops trying to escape. Wounded soldiers could get airlifted to safety.

The Huey was the most common helicopter. It could do many jobs. Often, one Huey would be loaded with troops. Another would be armed with missiles and machine guns. The helicopters would work together.

Observation helicopters flew low. Pilots searched for the enemy in the jungle. A fighter helicopter called the Snake would follow. The Snake launched rockets when the enemy was spotted. The US called their strategy the "air assault."

12,000 Number of helicopters used by the United States in the Vietnam War.

Cargo helicopters carried 55 soldiers and heavy equipment. • The "Jolly Green Giant" flew long distances. It could refuel in mid-air. • Skycranes lifted helicopters and airplanes that had been shot down.

Two restored Vietnam-era Huey helicopters take part in an air show.

Soldiers rappel down from a helicopter.

GROWING INFLUENCE

The Viet Cong had an unusual way of fighting. It was called **guerrilla warfare**. They carried out small attacks. They set traps and land mines along roads. They planted bombs in towns where US troops stayed. Sometimes, they followed their enemies as closely as possible. This meant air strikes could not be carried out. Americans did not want to risk harming their own troops.

US Attacks the Ho Chi Minh *Trail*

6

The Ho Chi Minh Trail connected North and South Vietnam. It was not a single path. It was a whole network. The main trail passed through Laos and Cambodia. Side trails led to South Vietnam. North Vietnam began using it in 1959. Weapons and food that traveled down the trail fed the Viet Cong. Troops followed the trail too. During the 1960s, the trail expanded. More troops and supplies traveled on it. Some trails led nowhere. These "dummy" trails confused US troops.

US military leaders wanted to stop people from using the trail. They decided to bomb parts of it. They called the mission Operation Rolling Thunder. It started on March 2, 1965. Bombing began north of the 17th Parallel. By 1966, there were targets across North Vietnam.

Next, President Johnson sent in ground forces. They were meant to defend the air bases. But they soon found themselves in active combat with the Viet Cong. China and the Soviet Union gave aid to North Vietnam. They were able to build an air defense system. They shot down hundreds of enemy planes. Many US troops were taken as prisoners of war.

People can still walk the Ho Chi Minh Trail.

12,000 Miles (19,312 kilometers) that made up the Ho Chi Minh Trail.

It took about a month to march from North Vietnam to South Vietnam. • The trail was used throughout the war. • More than 1 million North Vietnamese soldiers used the trail.

A US helicopter drops Agent Orange over Vietnam.

CHEMICAL WEAPONS The Ho Chi Minh Trail was in the middle of a jungle. Helicopters flew overhead. But US troops could not see through the trees. They sprayed the jungle with Agent Orange. This chemical killed plants. It revealed hiding places. But it also destroyed crops. US troops used **napalm** bombs. The chemical mixture burned fast. One bomb could kill a large section of the jungle.

Viet Cong Go *Underground*

7

In December 1965, Ho Chi Minh changed his military strategy. His army would no longer fight head-on. Guerrilla warfare was more effective. The army used traps and land mines. It also had weapons from the Soviet Union and China.

The Viet Cong wanted to hide their bases. In the jungle, they used the forest as cover. The leafy trees hid them. Hiding in cities was harder. The Viet Cong went underground. A network of tunnels gave them a place to hide. Like the Ho Chi Minh Trail, they used the tunnels to move troops and supplies. The tunnels crisscrossed the country. They let Viet Cong spy on the enemy. US troops swarmed the ground above. But the Viet Cong were hidden underneath. They planned and launched attacks.

Vietnamese landmine

The underground tunnels from the war are now a historic place to visit.

LIVING UNDERGROUND

In some places, entire villages lived in underground shelters. The shelters had all the things people needed to survive. They had kitchens and hospitals. Some even had weapons factories. Sometimes, there were places for villagers to gather. They could go to underground theaters and music halls.

One of the largest tunnel networks was beneath the Cu Chi district. It was northwest of the capital of South Vietnam. These tunnels linked soldiers as far away as the Cambodian border. The tunnels were narrow. Many Americans could not fit. Some were trained to be "tunnel rats." They had to enter one at a time. They scouted the underground maze. They warned troops above about traps.

5.4 Maximum height in feet (1.6 meters) for tunnel rats.

Troops had to be willing to crawl in dark, narrow spaces. • Some were down there for a long time. • Soldiers left helmets and coats behind before they went in.

A tourist tries to fit into the narrow tunnel.

North Vietnam Launches the *Tet Offensive*

8

In 1968, the Lunar New Year began on January 29. In Vietnam, the holiday is called Tet. Throughout the war, both sides stopped fighting on Tet. This let everyone celebrate. Most South Vietnamese troops had gone home to their families.

At midnight, fireworks were set off to welcome the new year. Just as the fireworks were ending, the North Vietnamese and Viet Cong made their move. It was a planned strike. More than 100 cities, villages, and bases were attacked at the same time. The US **embassy** was also part of the attack.

US army leaders were stunned. It had taken the North Vietnamese and Viet Cong months to move into position. Yet the United States had not seen the attack coming. People saw it as an intelligence failure.

North Vietnamese General Vo Nguyen Giap was in charge. His troops fought fiercely. They were successful at first. But his forces were spread too thin. US and South Vietnamese forces pushed them back. The battle was over as quickly as it began.

It was a major military defeat for North Vietnam. But it was also a political defeat for the United States.

64 Number of district capitals attacked in the Tet Offensive.

Giap led around 70,000 North Vietnamese troops into battle. • Around 12,500 civilians died. • North Vietnam wanted South Vietnam to rebel against US troops.

Americans had not realized that North Vietnam was capable of such an attack. President Johnson had promised that the war's end was near. But people saw that the war would not be over quickly. Many Americans withdrew their support of the war effort.

THINK ABOUT IT

Compare and contrast the policies of US presidents, from Eisenhower to Nixon. How did their views change the course of the war?

South Vietnamese soldiers defend Saigon during the Tet Offensive.

Antiwar Movement Grows in *the United States*

9

Antiwar **protests** in the United States started small. Most took place on college campuses. The protesters said that they did not feel threatened by a communist Vietnam. They spoke out against President Johnson. They thought he should not support the South Vietnamese government.

By 1967, the movement had grown. On October 21, an antiwar march took place in Washington, DC. People wanted to raise awareness for peace. Around 100,000 protesters met near the Lincoln **Memorial**. Later, 35,000 marched on the Pentagon. They clashed with police. Nearly 700 of them were arrested.

Johnson did not run for re-election in 1968. Richard Nixon took office in January 1969. He did not listen to the protesters. He called them a "vocal **minority**." He believed that most Americans were for the war.

At that time, young men had to sign up for military service. They were **drafted**. On December 1, 1969, Nixon began the draft **lottery**. All men aged 18 to 26 could be picked to join the war effort. They would be called into service based on their birthdates.

The draft was not popular. Many of those drafted were against the war. Some were proud to serve. But they wanted jobs away from the frontlines. They hoped for jobs in offices. Others dodged the draft. They faked medical conditions. Others fled to Canada.

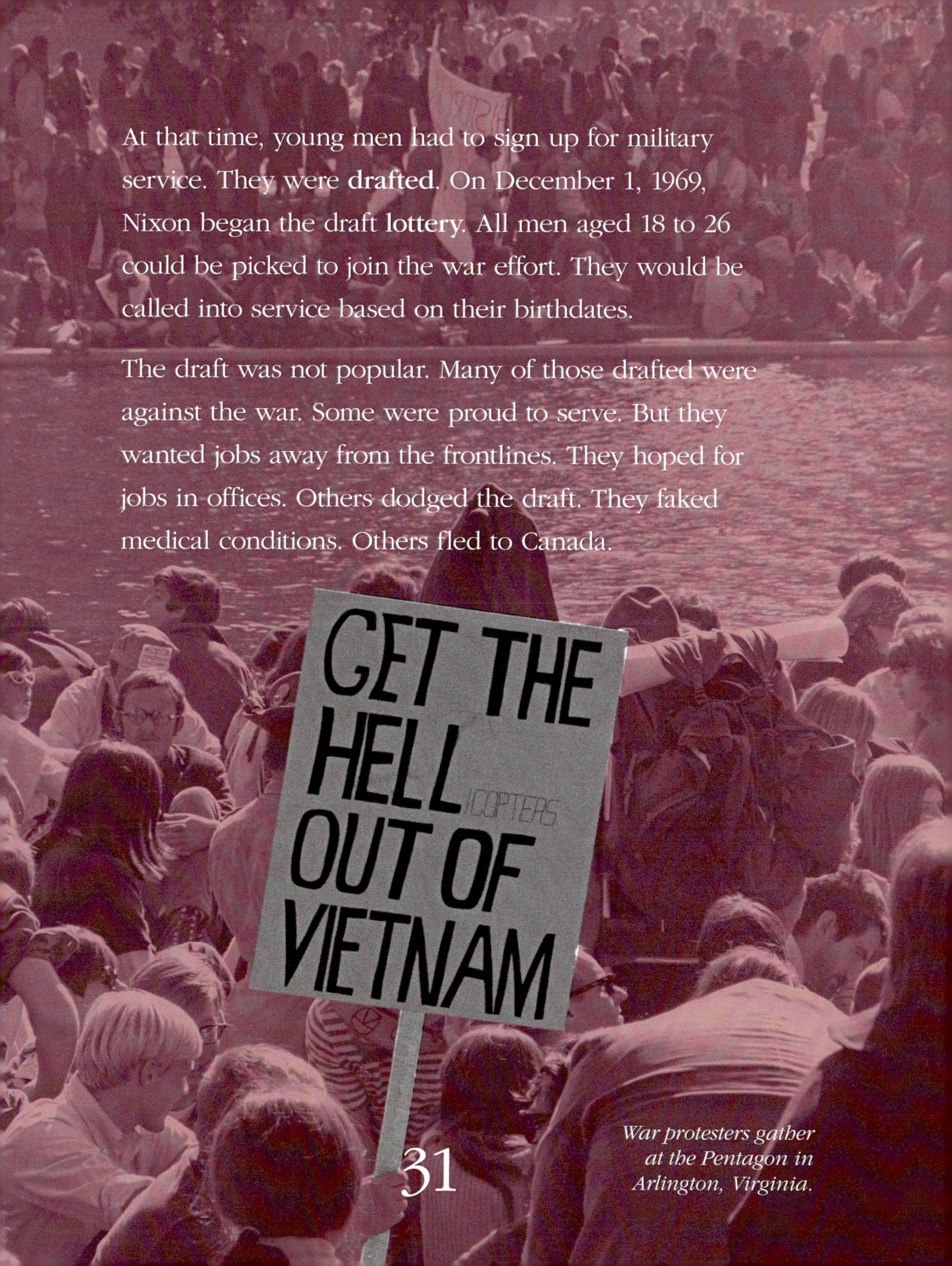

War protesters gather at the Pentagon in Arlington, Virginia.

THINK ABOUT IT Americans had different opinions about the war. If you lived during that time, would you support or protest it?

SELECTIVE SERVICE SYSTEM

NOTICE OF CLASSIFICATION

This is to certify that

Todd	S.	Strand
(First name)	(Middle initial)	(Last name)

Selective Service No.

32	35	51	4

is classified in Class II-S

until 10-15-72

by Local Board unless otherwise checked below:

☐ by Appeal Board

vote of ________ to ________

☐ by President

____

(Date of mailing)

____

(Member, Executive Secretary, or clerk of local board)

____

(Registrant's signature)

SSS Form 110 (Rev. 5-25-67)
(Previous printings are obsolete)
(Approval not required)

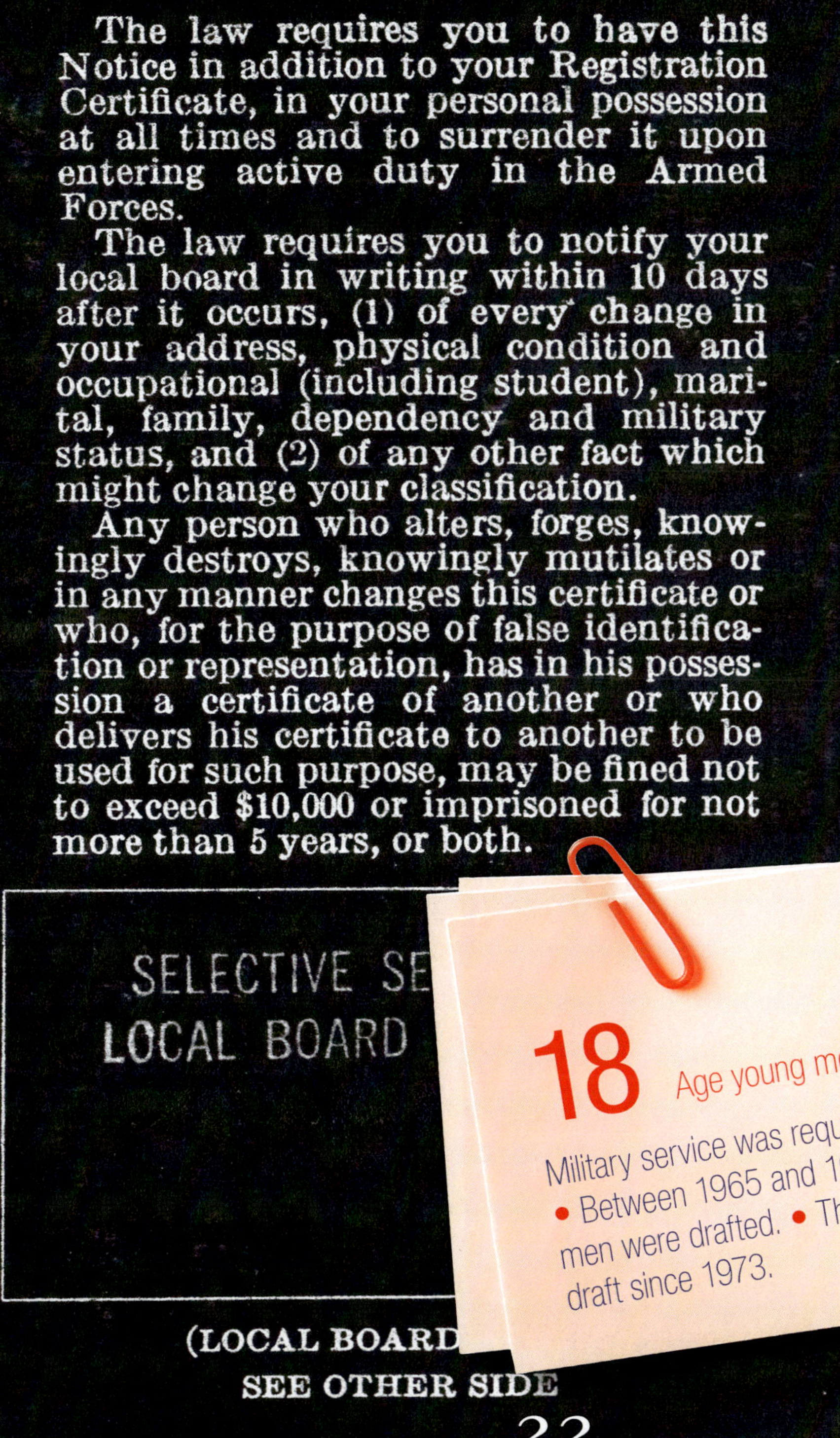
The law requires you to have this Notice in addition to your Registration Certificate, in your personal possession at all times and to surrender it upon entering active duty in the Armed Forces.

The law requires you to notify your local board in writing within 10 days after it occurs, (1) of every change in your address, physical condition and occupational (including student), marital, family, dependency and military status, and (2) of any other fact which might change your classification.

Any person who alters, forges, knowingly destroys, knowingly mutilates or in any manner changes this certificate or who, for the purpose of false identification or representation, has in his possession a certificate of another or who delivers his certificate to another to be used for such purpose, may be fined not to exceed $10,000 or imprisoned for not more than 5 years, or both.

SELECTIVE SE

LOCAL BOARD

(LOCAL BOARD

SEE OTHER SIDE

Draft cards noted a man's name, age, and draft status.

18 Age young men could be drafted.

Military service was required. It was not voluntary. • Between 1965 and 1973, about 1.7 million men were drafted. • The country has not had a draft since 1973.

Saigon Falls to the *North Vietnamese*

10

President Nixon was stuck fighting a war no one wanted. He made a new policy. The United States would train the South Vietnamese. They would send weapons. Then, the Vietnamese could fight on their own.

The United States planned to pull troops from combat. They started in 1969. For the first time in years, the number of men leaving was greater than the number arriving. The last American ground forces left Vietnam in March 1973.

The United States sent less other military aid after that. Without support, South Vietnam had a hard time. The North Vietnamese marched south. They claimed new territory. They headed toward Saigon, the capital of South Vietnam.

Gerald Ford was elected president in 1974. Ford asked Congress to send military aid to South Vietnam. Congress did not believe the South could win. They only sent some

20 Number of years the Vietnam War lasted.

Much of Vietnam had been destroyed by bombs and chemicals. • Land mines were hidden throughout the country. • Thousands of people fled South Vietnam by boat in 1975 and 1978.

US soldiers returning from the war did not receive a big welcome.

aid. It was not as much as Ford was hoping. Most aid was used to rescue Americans and some South Vietnamese from Saigon. Many more South Vietnamese were left behind. Hundreds of thousands of them boarded boats. They tried to flee. They were afraid of the new government. The boats were crowded. They were attacked by pirates. Many people got sick or died. Some drowned.

Saigon fell on April 30, 1975. South Vietnam surrendered. Saigon was renamed Ho Chi Minh City. The two parts of Vietnam were reunited. It was now the Socialist Republic of Vietnam.

South Vietnam staffers sign their surrender in April 1975.

11

Refugees Flee as Vietnam *Recovers*

After the war, Vietnam was in ruins. Those left behind had to pick up the pieces. Bombing and ground fighting had destroyed whole cities and villages. Forests were gone. Roads were damaged. During the war, bombs had been used to make them impossible to drive across. This stopped enemies moving supplies or people. But now people could not use the roads. They had to find other paths. Land mines were hidden across the country. Some were as small as a bullet. Anyone who stepped on one could be seriously injured. They might even die.

Many in South Vietnam were not happy. The people who had fought against the North were in danger. Anyone who had helped the Americans could be punished. The communist leaders executed around 65,000 Vietnamese after the war. Another million were sent to prison camps.

Ho Chi Minh had died in 1969. Ton Duc Thang replaced him. Under the new government, leaving the country was illegal. Still, people tried to escape. They packed onto fishing boats and other small vessels.

Those who made it out resettled in other countries. Many fled to the United States, Australia, and Canada. For them, the war meant having to leave their homes. For those who stayed, it meant living in a new communist Vietnam.

DEATH AND DESTRUCTION Most of the fighting took place in South Vietnam. But the United States dropped bombs in both the north and south. Agent Orange and napalm burns stretched across the jungles. Agent Orange destroyed 4.5 million acres (1.8 million hectares) of land. It also harmed people. The toxic chemicals caused cancer and other long-term health issues.

Agent Orange caused birth defects and other health disorders.

Many people had to cram together on planes or ships to escape Vietnam.

3.3 million Number of Vietnamese people who died in the war.

This number includes 2 million Vietnamese civilians. • Three million Vietnamese were wounded. • Two million became refugees.

12 The War Is Considered *a US Loss*

Vietnam was the first foreign war where the United States failed to reach its goals. It tried to stop communism. In the end, South Vietnam fell to communism anyway.

The war effort was also very expensive. It cost billions of dollars. This hurt the US economy for years. Prices raised. The country struggled. An oil shortage during the 1970s made it worse. Americans grew distrustful of entering foreign wars.

After the World Wars, troops had come home to parades. They were treated as heroes. But Americans did not see Vietnam veterans in the same way. Antiwar protesters did not think kindly of the soldiers. Women who served were not respected. Injured soldiers felt lost and alone. Even supporters of the war did not welcome the soldiers home.

Still, a memorial was built in Washington, DC. The Vietnam Veterans Memorial was dedicated on November 13, 1982. It is made of black granite. It lists all the US soldiers who died or went missing. There are more than 58,000 names. Over time, most Americans' feelings toward the veterans changed. They felt the soldiers deserved respect. They had, after all, served their country.

The Vietnam War cost about $760 billion.

The Vietnam Memorial is near the Washington Monument.

2.6 million Number of US men and women who served in Vietnam.

Many veterans struggled with trauma. • They had a hard time with mental health issues. • Many had health problems from the chemicals used in the war.

Think About It Look at other American wars. How did the Vietnam War affect support for these wars?

12 Key Dates

March 12, 1947
US President Harry S. Truman announces the Truman Doctrine. He promises US aid to countries threatened by communism.

July 21, 1954
The Geneva Accords divide Vietnam into two countries.

August 2, 1964
North Vietnam attacks the US destroyer *Maddox* in the Gulf of Tonkin.

August 4, 1964
President Lyndon B. Johnson receives reports attacks on two US destroyers.

August 7, 1964
Congress approves the Gulf of Tonkin Resolution.

March 2, 1965
The US Army launches Operation Rolling Thunder.

March 12, 1947

April 2, 1964

October 21, 1967
About 100,000 people march in an antiwar protest in Washington, DC.

January 31, 1968
The Viet Cong and North Vietnamese launch the Tet Offensive.

December 1, 1969
President Richard Nixon begins the draft lottery.

March 29, 1973
The last US ground forces leave Vietnam.

April 30, 1975
Saigon falls to North Vietnam.

November 13, 1982
The Vietnam Veteran Memorial is dedicated.

October 21, 1982

December 1, 1969

November 13, 1982

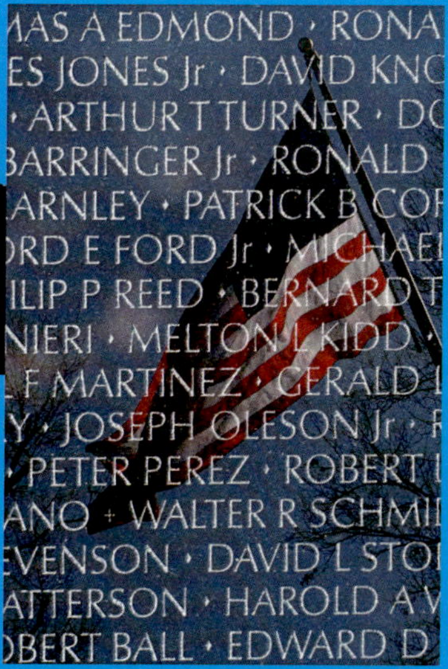

Glossary

aid
Help or assistance that is given to someone in need.

air strike
An attack in which military planes drop bombs.

assassinate
To kill someone important or famous for political reasons.

communist
To be a part of a system of government in which all property is controlled by the government.

doctrine
A statement of government policy especially in international relations.

draft
A system that requires people to join the military for a period of time.

embassy
The building where an ambassador lives and works.

guerrilla warfare
A form of military fighting where small groups of fighters attack fast and work independently.

international waters
The areas of the sea that are beyond any countries' coastline.

lottery
A system used to decide who will get something by choosing names and numbers randomly.

memorial
Something that honors a person or people who have died.

minority
A member of a group of people who are different from the larger group in a country or area.

napalm
A thick substance that has gasoline and is used in bombs to create a fire that burns hot and strong over a wide area.

protest
Words or actions that show disagreement.

reform
To improve something by removing or correcting problems.

resolution
A formal statement that expresses the feelings or decision of a groupt.

revolution
An attempt by many people to end the rule of a government.

For More Information

Books

Monroe, Alex. *The Vietnam War*. Minneapolis: Bellwether, 2024.

O'Conner, Jim. *What Was the Vietnam War?* New York: Penguin Workshop, 2019.

Rebman, Nick. *The Cold War*. Mendota Heights, MN: Focus Readers, 2024.

Websites

Vietnam Veterans Memorial
www.defense.gov/Multimedia/Experience/Vietnam-Veterans-Memorial/

Vietnam War
kids.britannica.com/students/article/Vietnam-War/277599

When Was the Vietnam War?
www.wonderopolis.org/wonder/When-Was-the-Vietnam-War

About the Author

Lori Dittmer has written more than 80 nonfiction books for children. She is passionate about creating books that inspire curiosity and a love for learning in young readers. She lives with her husband in southern Minnesota. In her free time, she enjoys reading, hiking, and going on adventures with her family.

Index

TOP RANK is published by Black Rabbit Books, P.O. Box 227, Mankato, MN, 56002. •

Copyright © 2026 Black Rabbit Books. All rights reserved. No part of this book may be reproduced in any form without written permission from the publisher. •

Designed by Danny Nanos • Photographs © Alamy Stock Photo/American Photo Archive, 39, Everett Collection, 23, J. G. Domke, 35, Todd Strand, 32–33; Associated Press/Sarah Errington, 34, 36; Dreamstime/Annette Rüppel, 24, Steve Mann, 11; Getty Images/Athanasios Gioumpasis, 18–19; Shutterstock/Belinda Pretorius, 48, Danita Delimont, 42–43, Duc Huy Nguyen, 2, 12, Efired, 6, J. Helgason, 14, John Keith, 45, Jolygon, 46–47, Keith Tarrier, 27, Lefteris Papaulakis, 30, OlegD, 26, Oliver Denker, cover, 1, Prachaya Roekdeethaweesab, 45, Rainer Lesniewski, 4, specnaz, 41, Vacclav, 40, Ververidis Vasilis, 17, 20, xuanhuongho, 22, 25, Zbitnev, 13, Zhenny-zhenny, 37; Wikimedia Commons/Alexis Duclos, 38, Frank Wolfe, 31, 45, Greta Kempton/Harry S. Truman Library, 7, 44, Naval History and Heritage Command NH 74165, 2–3, 8–9, Photographer's Mate 3rd Class Ramon Preciado, 15, public domain, 10, U.S. Air Force, 10, U.S. Navy Bureau of Ships, 16, 44, USAF, 38, US Information Agency, 5, US military personnel, 28–29

Library of Congress Cataloging-in-Publication Data: Names: Dittmer, Lori author | Title: The Vietnam War: 12 things to know / by Lori Dittmer. | Description: Mankato, MN: Black Rabbit Books, [2026] | Series: America at war | Includes bibliographical references and index. | Grades 4–6 | Ages 9–13 | Identifiers: LCCN 2024050089 | ISBN 9781644668559 (paperback) | ISBN 9781644668238 (library binding) | ISBN 9781644668870 (ebook) | Subjects: LCSH: Vietnam War, 1961–1975—Juvenile literature | Vietnam War, 1961–1975—United States—Juvenile literature | Classification: LCC DS557.7 .D58 2026 | DDC 959.704/3—dc23/eng | LC record available at https://lccn.loc.gov/2024050089